King Ar
Footsteps

Paul White

Bossiney Books · Launceston

First published 2002 by
Bossiney Books, Langore,
Launceston. Cornwall PL15 8LD
www.bossineybooks.com
This reprint 2005
ISBN 1-899383-52-2

Acknowledgements
The artwork on the cover and
title page is by Sharon Keogh.
The illustration on page 2 and the
maps are by Graham Hallowell.
The photograph on page 13 is by
permission of Cornish Picture
Library/Paul Watts. All other
photographs are by the author.

Printed in Great Britain by
R Booth Ltd, Mabe, Cornwall

An artist's impression of the gateway of a large post-Roman hill-fort

Introduction

It is well known that the King Arthur of medieval literature may have been based on a real person, who might or might not have been a king and who probably flourished around AD 500-550, in the period of British history known to archaeologists and historians as 'post-Roman', but popularly known as 'the Dark Ages'.

In an earlier book, *King Arthur, Man or Myth?*, I tried to summarise what evidence there is for this 'real' Arthur, but the evidence is far from easy to interpret and is certainly not enough to prove he existed. My conclusion was that we are unlikely ever to be sure that a real Arthur lived, but that quite probably he did; and that if he lived then it was almost certainly in Dumnonia, which was a tribal territory covering Cornwall, Devon and part of Somerset.

In this book I shall be assuming that 'Arthur' did in fact exist, and visiting places in the South-West which have an Arthurian connection of one kind or another. I hope readers will be inspired to follow.

There are no buildings of this period left – they were mainly timber constructions and have long since rotted away – but there are numerous earthworks, particularly hill-forts. In the South-West alone there are hundreds of earthworks, most of them dating from the Iron Age (the centuries before the Roman conquest in AD43) and only a few of them are known to have been re-used in the post-Roman period (after AD410), but that may be because relatively few have been excavated.

Some of the places mentioned in this book are very beautiful and a joy to visit in their own right, regardless of Arthur; some are evocative of the post-Roman period and encourage the imagination to run free; but inevitably a few are disappointing and (except for the committed Arthur enthusiast) not really worth the effort of a visit. I can do no more than indicate which have given me most pleasure and hope you share my enjoyment of some immensely attractive places, mostly in Cornwall and Somerset.

'King Arthur's grave' – or a medieval fake – at Glastonbury Abbey

The context

The Romans administered Dumnonia as a *civitas* (something like a 'Unitary Local Authority' in modern terms) and they did so from Exeter (*Isca Dumnoniorum*, 'Isca of the Dumnonians'). It had its own local senate which was dominated by the rich and powerful, who were Romanised Britons, not colonising Italians. They were landed gentry, with a country estate or estates and a large town house in Isca.

When Britannia ceased to be a part of the Roman Empire around AD 410, central power within Britain immediately disappeared and each *civitas* assumed power in its own area. At first the local bigwigs relished their independence. Losing the *pax Romana* was a bit of a worry, but losing the tax Romana made up for it – the Empire had milked its provinces dry to pay for its over-extended armies and for imperial luxury.

But before long there were internal dissensions between the *civitates* as well as continued attacks and intrusions – not just from the Saxons but from the Irish who had settled in South Wales and had then set their sights on Dumnonia. The economy worsened, money gave way to barter, there were crop failures and plagues. Many Dumnonians emigrated to Brittany, which was underpopulated. The British population may have fallen by as much as two-thirds. The Roman towns were abandoned (the walls too extensive to defend and their infrastructure in terminal decay) and ancient hill-forts, some of them the size of a small town, were refortified after 400 years of disuse.

Under such pressures the local oligarchy often gave way to an autocratic system under a ruler, who in time acquired the title of king, in Latin *tyrannus* (from which comes our word tyrant) rather than the word for a legitimate king, *rex*.

To add to the confusion there were religious differences. Christianity had been the official religion of the Roman Empire since AD 312 but in Britain was confined mainly to the upper classes and to the 'lowland zone' – roughly south and east of the

Opposite: Arthurian sites in Cornwall

4

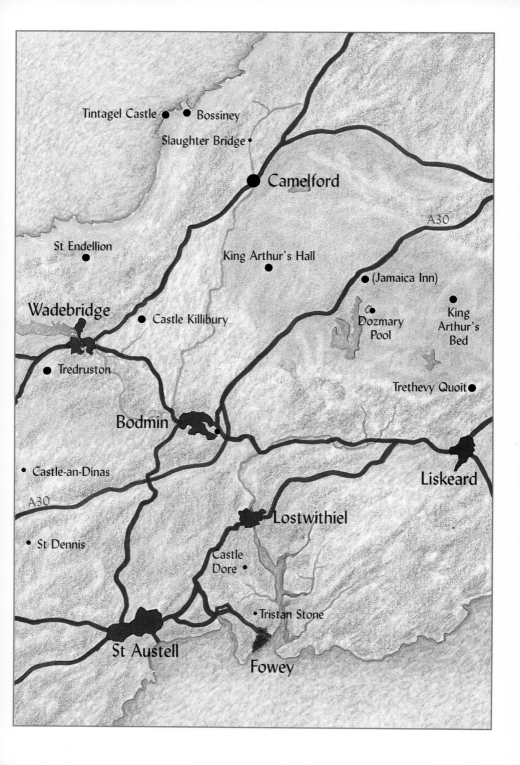

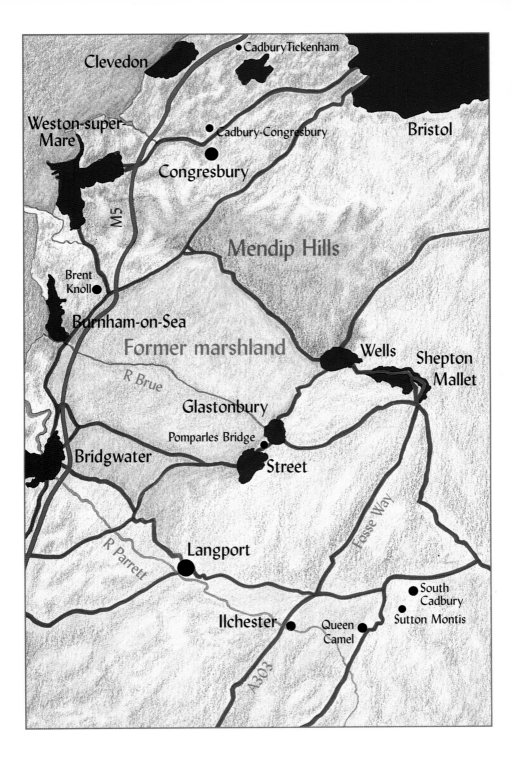

Fosse Way. The *pagani* (countryfolk) remained 'pagan'. Even among the upper classes there is little evidence that Dumnonia had widely accepted Christianity in the Roman period.

When the Christians did move in, from about 450-500 and possibly as immigrant landowners rather than as missionaries in the modern sense, they came from different directions: the 'Celtic Christianity' imported by the Irish, by way of South Wales, was often at odds with the Roman church, supported by those who wanted to reunite Britannia with Rome. Many of the British followed the beliefs of one of their number, Pelagius, whose thinking was far too sensible for the theologians: he was declared a heretic in 417. And then along came the Saxons, bringing their own different 'paganism'.

Can we imagine the chaos created by all these social forces? In our own time we have seen the collapse of the Soviet empire, and then that of Yugoslavia. That may help us visualise post-Roman Britannia, a coherent state falling into its constituent parts and riddled by local nationalisms and religious and cultural differences, all fuelled by the ambitions of rival warlords.

Was Arthur a 'warlord'? Certainly he was described by a later writer as fighting 'with the kings of the Britons but he himself was *dux bellorum*'. *Dux bellorum* literally means 'leader of wars', perhaps 'commander-in-chief'. Was he a Christian? Not necessarily: many of the Welsh sources suggest he was at odds with the churchmen of his time. Was he a good man and a noble leader? Who knows. In tough times a Hitler or a Slobodan Milosevic may be popular with his own people, whatever their neighbours, or 'History', may think of him.

And there is no doubt from the reputation Arthur left behind that his own people, particularly in the South-West, remembered him as a great war leader who had won many battles, probably fought in different parts of Britain, and had stemmed the tide of foreign encroachments. In particular he was remembered as defeating the Saxons decisively by a great victory at the battle of Badon.

Opposite: Arthurian sites in Somerset

The marshes, now drained, formed a natural defence for Dumnonia

But in the long run the Saxon (English-speaking) kingdoms could not be kept at arm's length. The boundary of Dumnonia was step by step driven back until it reached the Tamar, after which only Cornwall remained and the name Dumnonia disappeared. The kingdom of Cornwall ceased to be independent in the ninth century but there are still many Cornish people for whom Cornwall is most definitely not part of England.

The Battle of Langport

There is a poem in Old Welsh which commemorates the death of Gereint, king of Dumnonia, in a battle at 'Llongborth', in which some of those fighting with Gereint are described as 'Arthur's brave men'.

There is much that is unclear about this fragment of ancient poetry. 'Llongborth' is probably Langport, which was on the natural border of Dumnonia, protected by the River Parrett and the extensive marshland. The photograph above was taken at Oath Lock, part of the massive modern drainage scheme which has reclaimed these lands, although even now widespread flooding is the norm in a bad winter. In ancient times, the marshes were grazing land in summer but totally impassable in winter. Langport is the easiest crossing point and therefore a likely place for a battle. The date of Gereint's death is not known.

It is highly unlikely that Arthur was present; he had probably already been dead for a century. 'Arthur's brave men' is a poetic phrase which to the audience would have suggested 'men of Dumnonia', though there may possibly have been a war-band which had taken Arthur's name.

Arthur's conception at Tintagel

Every legendary hero in the ancient world had to have a mysterious birth. It was assumed that any person destined for secular or religious greatness would have been marked out by special circumstances at their birth, so the myth-makers invented and embroidered the events of their hero's nativity.

The first writer whose work survives to tell us about Arthur in any detail was Geoffrey of Monmouth, a cleric writing around 1135. Geoffrey was either Breton (as were many of those who came over with William the Conqueror) or Welsh, or possibly even Cornish. It is unclear what proportion of his *History* Geoffrey invented himself but he may have had access, as he claimed, to earlier writings or oral traditions in the Celtic languages which neither the Saxons nor the Normans would have known about. If so, he certainly 'improved on' his sources.

The story Geoffrey tells is a long way from an immaculate conception – indeed it is by modern standards a sordid tale! – and it involves named places in Cornwall.

Gorlois, Duke of Cornwall brings his wife to court, where King Uther Pendragon lusts after her – so very publicly that the Duke beats a hasty retreat, taking his wife Igerna (or Ingerna) with him. The king is furious and demands their return. When Gorlois refuses, Uther invades Cornwall. Gorlois puts Igerna into his castle of Tintagel and himself goes to 'Dimilioc'.

While Uther's army besieges Dimilioc, the king persuades Merlin to give him a magic disguise to enable him to pretend to be Gorlois. The disguise is so successful that Uther walks straight past the guards, has a candle-lit supper with Igerna and hops happily into the nuptial bed. Arthur is conceived that night. And despite what you might think, he isn't illegitimate because, while these goings on were going on, Gorlois got himself killed sallying out of Dimilioc. So Uther weds the widow and all (in Geoffrey's clerical mind) is well.

An American lady visiting Tintagel, who had not heard the story before, exclaimed to me 'But that's rape!' Which perhaps it was – if it ever happened, which is highly unlikely. But if it did happen then perhaps what we are getting is the post-Roman equivalent of a spin-doctor at work. Perhaps Igerna *liked* the attention she received from the king and was furious at being dragged from a good party by her boring old husband. Perhaps she fancied being queen and she and her entourage knew only too well whom they let into the castle that night. It would not be without parallel in either history or west-country legend.

But the truth is more likely to be that someone, either Geoffrey or an earlier writer, borrowed an ancient Greek myth and gave it a Cornish setting. The God Zeus took the form of

These remains of the living quarters of a post-Roman stronghold at Tintagel were heavily restored in the 1930s

The Island at Tintagel, probable site of a post-Roman royal citadel

Amphitryon to seduce Amphitryon's wife Alcmena, who gave birth to Heracles (Hercules). So the British hero shares his birth-story with the Greek demi-god.

Although Tintagel is often said to have been Arthur's birthplace, Geoffrey states only that Arthur was conceived there. Royal households in those days, and indeed until the seventeenth century, moved around the kingdom. Apart from impressing people with the trappings of power, it was easier to take the household to a series of food-sources rather than to bring food to one central location. So nine months later Uther and Igerna might have been anywhere in their kingdom.

Until the 1990s it was believed that the 'Island' at Tintagel was the site of a Celtic monastery, but recent excavations have demolished this idea and shown Tintagel to have been a secular site in the post-Roman period. So much imported Mediterranean pottery has been found here that it is clear it was a very high status site, probably a citadel of the Cornish (or perhaps Dumnonian) royal family of the time. This discovery came as a

Of all the places in this book, Tintagel to my mind is the most beautiful. Do not be put off by the hectic nature of the village itself. Give yourself enough time to approach the castle from St Merteriana's church (itself well worth a visit) and then do visit the castle (English Heritage, fee) because it really is very fine – not so much the crumbling walls of the medieval castle (built in the 1230s) as the dramatic setting.

The cave at the foot of the cliff is 'Merlin's Cave' (see pages 31-32)

shock to those who believe Geoffrey to have been just a romancer, because what seemed undoubtedly fictional now could, just could, have some basis in fact.

Another blow for a historical Arthur connection seemed to have been struck when a piece of slate incised with the name ARTOGNOU, which apparently would have been pronounced 'Arthnoo', was found in a sixth century context at Tintagel. Scholars however have proved hard to convince that the stone refers to our Arthur.

Castle-an-Dinas, a major Iron Age hill-fort

Dimilioc

While Igerna was entertaining Uther at Tintagel, her husband Gorlois was at 'Dimilioc' which was presumably another hill fort, probably Iron Age in origin and renovated in the post-Roman period. So where was Dimilioc?

One candidate, according to the historian Charles Henderson, is Castle-an-Dinas, just to the north of Goss Moor on the A30 (Cornish Heritage Trust, free). This massive Iron Age fort is definitely worth a visit: its ramparts are clearly defined and (unlike some other hill-forts) clear of trees – but there is no evidence as yet that it was re-used in the post-Roman period.

The reason, I suspect, is its sheer size. The outer ramparts are some 800 m long. How many warriors would be needed to defend them? More than Gorlois had at his disposal I imagine.

In their heyday, these hill-forts would have been much more impressive than they are today: soil has inevitably eroded from

St Dennis – a church within an ancient hill-fort

the ramparts into the ditches. In many cases the bank was fronted by stonework, long since robbed away or covered by the eroding earth, and of course the ramparts were topped by timber palisades.

Just 3 km south of Castle-an-Dinas lies another smaller fort – St Dennis, which got its name by a corruption of the Cornish word *dinas*, a hill-fort, not from the French saint Dennis, who was only introduced to make sense of the name. The churchyard itself defines the area of the fort. St Dennis lies in the china clay district, usually avoided by tourists unless on their way to the Eden Project, but personally I would recommend a trip to this place, which has a unique character. And if you leave the church and head towards Indian Queens on the B3279 you will pass (immediately west of a narrow bridge over the former railway) Domellick Manor and Domellick Farm. Surely St Dennis is the real Dimilioc, as Geoffrey envisaged it? But if so, did Geoffrey take the name 'Dimilioc' from an earlier source, or had he, like any good fiction writer, looked around in Cornwall for a convincing location for his plot?

Dunster, near Minehead, a medieval town which should not be missed

Arthur's youth

It is a curious fact that while Tintagel and Glastonbury exploit their Arthur connections for all they are worth, another place in the South-West which has an excellent claim to Arthur seems commercially quite unaware of the fact!

A *Life of St Carantoc* (or Carranog) tells us that 'In those days Cato (Cadwy) and Arthur reigned in that country, living in Din-draithou.' And Dindraithou has been identified with Dunster.

The story involves Arthur looking for a monstrous dragon, which had been befriended by the saint. Arthur and Cadwy wanted to kill the dragon, which had been laying waste to 'Carrum' (Carhampton). The saint instead sends the dragon away, telling it never to hurt anyone again, and in return receives land at Carhampton, not to mention the return of his mobile altar, which Arthur had purloined and would have turned into a table, except that his sacrilegious tankards and plates kept being hurled off it onto the ground.

Many saints' *Lives* are excuses for explaining how a particular monastery or church came to own a certain property, and this one may have been written at the behest of Wells Cathedral, which had an interest in land hereabouts. What is interesting in this *Life*, however, is that Arthur is such a low-key figure – a joint ruler (and probably the junior partner at that) in one small part of Dumnonia. This seems to me to argue for its authenticity, since the writer could have raised St Carantoc's standing by having him come off best in a meeting with a great legendary king, rather than with a gauche lad called Arthur.

Carhampton has the misfortune of a really busy main road running through it, but Dunster is a superb little medieval town, preserved because it lost its historic trading importance when the harbour silted up. High above the town, with beautiful views across to Wales, is Bat's Castle, an Iron Age hill-fort. Was this perhaps where Cadwy and Arthur lived and ruled?

A second Welsh *Life* from the same time and area is *The Life of St Gildas* by Caradoc of Lancafarn. In this it is stated that Gildas was a contemporary of Arthur, who was king of the whole of Greater Britain (as opposed presumably to Brittany). Gildas was a real historical character who wrote the only British book to survive from the period, in which he tiresomely fails to mention Arthur! From the *Life* it appears that Gildas and Arthur were not on the best of terms, which could account for the omission. (Though another possible explanation is that Arthur never existed.)

In this *Life*, Gildas travels to Glastonbury Abbey at a time when Melwas is king of 'the summer region' – Somerset, which was possibly so named because the Moors and Levels provided wonderful summer grazing, but in winter were almost entirely under water.

Glastonbury was being besieged by 'the *tyrannus* Arthur with an innumerable multitude' because the wicked king Melwas had raped and abducted Guinevere, and brought her to an invulnerable place, protected by reeds and rivers and marshes. Arthur had searched for his queen 'through the cycle of a year' before he found where she was hidden, and then summoned the armies of Devon and Cornwall to his assistance.

Glastonbury Tor, visible for great distances across the flat lands, has always attracted legends and myth-makers

This looks rather like a pagan fertility myth converted into an Arthurian story, particularly with the phrase 'through the cycle of a year', but if there is any vestige of a historical event here, it would fit with Arthur as a local ruler in the east of Dumnonia, perhaps based at Dunster, and Melwas as king of the neighbouring state, with the marshes of the Rivers Brue and Parrett as a buffer between them. Arthur is able to call on forces from the whole of Dumnonia in his hour of need: probably he is a young relative of the king of Dumnonia.

Archaeology has shown that on the top of Glastonbury Tor there was a post-Roman settlement, but its function was unclear. The excavator, Philip Rahtz, thought the most likely use was as 'the stronghold of a local chieftain, an eyrie type fortress' – in other words the ideal place for the wicked Melwas to hide the abducted Guinevere!

Not all Arthurian sites are romantic or visually glamorous! This is Kelly Rounds, which has a claim to be no less a place than Camelot!

Camelot

There never was any such place outside the legends, of course, but if Arthur lived then he must have had one or more bases from which to operate.

Welsh sources place Arthur's headquarters at 'Celliwig' in Cornwall. The '-wig' probably represents the Latin *vicus*, pronounced 'weekus' in Britain, which implied a village or sometimes the settlement of camp-followers beside a fort; there are a number of places called Week in the South-West, and the element '-wick' is also found in many English place names.

'Celliwig' has been inconclusively identified with a large earthwork 2 km north-east of Wadebridge sometimes called Castle Killibury, sometimes Kelly Rounds. A farm called Kelly is nearby.

You can park on the A39 opposite Three Holes Cross, from which the earthwork is only a short walk. A bridleway runs through the middle of the fort, which has two encircling ramparts and is about 200 m across. To the north of the bridleway the ramparts and ditches are fairly well preserved, but nothing is visible of the southern half. Crop marks outside the ramparts have shown there were once 'annexes' which perhaps housed the *vicus*. A few fragments of *amphorae* have been found at the site, suggesting post-Roman occupation. Sadly this is not the most majestic hill-fort in the West, but if you really want to tread in Arthur's footsteps you should visit Kelly *vicus*.

Another hill-fort which just might be 'Celliwig' is Castle

Walking up the steep hill into South Cadbury hill-fort. Many of these sites involve some walking, at times quite strenuous

Canyke on the outskirts of Bodmin, which is 2km south of a property called Callywith. Castle Canyke was huge, surrounded by a single ditch. Not much remains to be seen.

South Cadbury

The traveller John Leland, writing in 1542, identified this major Somerset hill-fort, just south of the A303 west of Wincanton, as Arthur's Camelot. A massive excavation in the 1960s demonstrated that it had a long and impressive history going back to 3000 BC. In the Iron Age it was the site of a town, defended by four massive ramparts. Around AD 70 it was sacked by the Romans, and the inhabitants slaughtered – presumably in punishment for an uprising. Later in the Roman period there is evidence of pilgrimages to a pagan temple on the hill-top.

The town was refurbished from about 470, perhaps following the evacuation of the Roman town of Ilchester. This occupation

South Cadbury is one of the most impressive sites in this book, and well worth a detour. The sheer scale of the ramparts and of the area enclosed is quite remarkable, and the scenery very attractive

It used sometimes to be claimed that the pretty village of Queen Camel near South Cadbury, formerly just plain 'Camel', was the site of Camelot

of the site lasted for at least the next 80 years. It seems to have been an administrative capital for the area, which was the home of the Durotriges tribe, rather than a military headquarters. In the late Saxon period it was reoccupied yet again.

The Arthurian connections, however, now look rather less secure than they did in the heady days of the excavations in the 1960s. They still rely on Leland's statement that:

> At South Cadbyri standith Camallate, sumtyme a famose toun or castelle. The people can tell nothing but that they have hard say that Arture much resortid to Camalat.

In addition to that statement, local folklore (often interesting but never a reliable source of evidence) apparently includes two place names for local features, King Arthur's Palace and King Arthur's Well, as well as a tradition that the hill is hollow and that Arthur and his knights are asleep within a cavern deep inside. (As the hill is limestone, it may well contain the cave if not the drowsy warriors.)

And there is a tradition that on a certain night of the year – exactly which night is disputed – the king and his men ride down in ghostly form to a ford at Sutton Montis, where their horses drink. It is possible to find the route down through the ramparts towards Sutton Montis, which leads to a stile into a field, but there is, as I understand it, no right of way beyond the stile.

Other Somerset hill forts

There are two other 'Cadbury' sites a little further north in Somerset, one at Congresbury and the other at Tickenham. Rosemary Clinch and Michael Williams in *King Arthur in Somerset* (Bossiney Books, 1987, now out of print) suggest an Arthurian connection for both, but the evidence seems slight.

Cadbury-Congresbury is known to have been occupied in the post-Roman period, and very probably Cadbury-Tickenham was too – but that does not in itself prove an Arthurian connection. Geoffrey Ashe, in *The Quest for Arthur's Britain* (Paladin 1971), suggests that the name Cadbury might come from 'Cadwy's bury', in which case all three Cadburys might be associated with Arthur's co-ruler at Dunster.

Cadbury-Congresbury and Cadbury-Tickenham (right) are both attractive enough places, but relatively unexciting and with only a weak Arthurian connection

The views from the top of Brent Knoll, both inland and across to Wales, are well worth the climb

In quite a different category is Brent Knoll, that extraordinary hill which rises from the Somerset Levels and overlooks Sedgemoor Services on the M5. A well signed and gravelled footpath leads from just behind the church in Brent Knoll village up to the top of the hill, from which the views are enormous.

As you climb the steep path, it is not obvious that there is an earthwork on top, but once you are there the defences are clearly visible. It is known that the Knoll was in use in Roman times, and that there was a *castellarium* or small fort on the summit in the thirteenth century. The humps and bumps on the summit are quite complex and defy easy understanding.

This site definitely deserves a visit, and if you are travelling up the M5, the wind on the exposed summit will wake you up far more effectively than a service station coffee.

It has been suggested that Brent Knoll could have formed part of a beacon chain between South Cadbury, Glastonbury Tor and Dinas Powys in Wales.

According to William of Malmesbury's *The Antiquities of Glastonbury*, Arthur sent off a young hopeful called Yder to prove himself against three giants at 'the Mount of the Ranae [frogs] now called Brentecnol', where the young man successfully slew the giants. When Arthur arrived, Yder appeared to be dead of his wounds. Blaming himself for the death, Arthur set 80 monks praying for the soul of Yder (who was actually not dead but subsequently recovered) and gave lands to the Abbey, including Brent and Polden. This version of the tale was not written by William of Malmesbury himself, but was added later in an attempt to prove that the Abbey had held the lands in question for centuries. It does however seem to be a story of Welsh origin, and therefore part of genuine Arthurian folk-lore, though probably originally not related to Brent Knoll.

Badon

Arthur's most famous battle, in which he may have pushed back the advance of the Saxon kingdoms, was at 'the hill of Badon'. This may have been at Solsbury Hill, just north of Batheaston near Bath, or it may have been at Liddington Castle near Swindon, both of them hill-forts. Readers from London and beyond may think of Bath and even Swindon as being in the South-West, but seen from my perspective in Cornwall they are so far north-east as to be almost in Geordie-land – and therefore outside the scope of this book!

The Tristan Legend

More than a third of Malory's *Le Morte d'Arthur* consists of the story of 'Sir Tristram' which is a Frenchified form of 'Tristan', itself probably an approximation to 'Drust' which is claimed to be a Pictish name – but which certainly was used in Cornwall also, as is demonstrated by the place-name Tredruston, 'Druston's farmstead', near Wadebridge.

The story of Tristan and Iseult seems to have been Cornish in origin, though some suspect that it may have originated further north, and, like many of the stories in Malory, it once had a quite independent existence before it was dragged by Malory's immediate predecessors into the Arthurian scene.

The Longstone just outside Fowey has the inscription: 'Drustanus, son of Cunomorus'. This Drustan may well have been the Tristan of legend, and Cunomorus (probably Cynfawr) may have been King Mark

The legend tells us that Tristan is the nephew of King Mark of Cornwall. He is sent to Ireland to bring back Mark's new young bride, Iseult, for an arranged dynastic marriage. On the way back Tristan and Iseult fall madly in love, which the story excuses by their having accidentally drunk a love potion intended for Iseult and Mark. The subsequent triangle is the source of great distress to all three of them. This plot is easy enough for us to relate to today, but for its medieval audience, in a society where arranged marriages were the norm, it struck such a chord that this became *the* great love story of the time, and it was told in many versions, the most interesting of which, because it is quite psychologically sophisticated for a medieval work, is by Gottfried von Strassburg (available in Penguin paperback).

24

Another version is by a minstrel named Béroul, who doesn't just set the story vaguely in Cornwall: he clearly knows in some detail the places he is writing about. Joy Wilson's book *Tristan and Iseult, A Cornish love story* (Bossiney Books, 1999) follows Béroul's version in some detail and can be thoroughly recommended to visitors to Cornwall as a fun way of finding some little known but very beautiful places. Béroul's text, of course, does not prove the historical existence of the characters in the story, or that they lived in Cornwall, only that the minstrel had a personal knowledge of these places.

But there is a strong possibility that King Mark and Tristan actually did exist, with the king having strongholds at Tintagel and at Castle Dore near Fowey, a small earthwork which is quite magical in May when it is a riot of wild flowers. On the outskirts of Fowey stands 'the Tristan stone', with an inscription suggesting that Drustanus was the son (not nephew) of Cunomorus, who has been identified as Marcus Cunomorus who is said, in a ninth century manuscript, to have simultaneously ruled in Dumnonia and in Domnonée, a region of Brittany full of Dumnonian emigrants.

Arthur's death

The final act of the Arthurian legend is a civil war, in which Arthur's opponent is Mordred (originally Modred) who is actually Arthur's son by his half-sister – although neither of them knew they were committing incest: it was just one of those traps the gods have in store for legendary personalities. At a last fateful battle, known as Camlann or Camblan, Arthur kills Modred, but receives a terrible wound himself. He asks Sir Bedivere to go and cast his sword Excalibur into a lake; when Bedivere does so, a mysterious arm emerges from the water to catch the sword, which is thus returned to the magic world from which it came.

Arthur does not die on stage, but is placed in a barge carrying three queens, who take him away to 'Avalon', where his wounds will be healed. There are clearly ancient pagan elements to this story: valuable offerings in lakes have become quite a routine find in pre-Roman archaeology, and in legends lakes often have

Slaughter Bridge near Camelford, probably the site of a real battle between the Cornish and the Saxons, was traditionally claimed as the site of the legendary battle of Camlann

One of many places where the sword Excalibur might have been returned to the Lady of the Lake – Dozmary Pool, high on Bodmin Moor in Cornwall

priestesses who represent the goddess of the place. Dead or dying heroes might well be taken away to the Isles of the Blessed.

Such a story naturally attracted rival locations. A rather dull river crossing not far from Tintagel called Slaughter Bridge was traditionally claimed as Camlann, because the river (more of a stream here) is the Camel. It does seem to have been the site of a battle in 823 (or 824 or 825 depending on the source) and it is likely that this gave rise to the legend, added to the fact that there is an inscribed memorial stone near the bridge. This was once, in a burst of wishful thinking, misinterpreted as a memorial to Arthur, but is actually the stone of an otherwise unknown Latinus, son of Magarus. There are other plausible candidates for Camlann outside the South-West.

The lake into which the sword was thrown has at least three locations in the West Country alone. Cornish tradition identifies Dozmary Pool not far from Jamaica Inn on Bodmin Moor. The poet Tennyson, who did so much to popularise the Arthurian legend in Victorian times, saw Loe Pool south of Helston and decided that must have been the spot. Both are attractive places to visit.

In Somerset there is Pomparles Bridge, said to be a corruption of Pont Perilous, which the inventive monks of Glastonbury identified as the site. It lies on the main road between Glastonbury and Street. The picturesque medieval bridge was knocked down in the early nineteenth century, and its modern successor is utilitarian in the extreme.

Glastonbury Abbey also laid a claim to be the burial place of Arthur and Guinevere. Their bones were dug up in 1191.

Unfortunately, there is very good reason to suppose that the monks faked this discovery, as they had already faked the discovery of the body of St Dunstan, not to mention numerous charters and other 'evidence' of their rights and possessions. Presumably the means were thought justified by the holy end, which was to pay for rebuilding the abbey after a disastrous fire. The 'discovery' of King Arthur's bones turned out to be a much more successful crowd puller than any of the Abbey's saintly relics, and the Arthur connection continues to attract people to this day.

The fact that the monks were rogues and the burial a trick (possibly suggested by King Henry II who wanted Arthur proven dead, not sleeping with his knights in a cave, awaiting the moment when he would drive both Normans and English out of Britain) should not stop you visiting Glastonbury. There is a great deal to attract even sceptical earth-bound Taureans like myself, and those with a spiritual leaning, Christian or otherwise, often find themselves bowled over by the experience.

Was there any historical Camlann, and if so was it as the legend describes it? A document generally called the *Welsh Annals* records that in AD 539 (probably!) there occurred 'The battle of Camlann in which Arthur and Medraut both fell, and there was a plague in Britain and Ireland.' The manuscript of the *Annals* was written many centuries after 539, and there is no way of knowing when this entry was first written down, but whoever wrote it believed the battle to be a historical event.

One intriguing aspect is what it does not say – that Arthur and Modred were on opposite sides. That may be a later invention. The name 'Modred' continued to be used in Cornwall, witness the village name Tremodrett near Goss Moor, whereas we might have expected the stain of Modred's treachery to have put it out of favour. So perhaps they fought on the same side, or perhaps – heretically – they were on opposite sides but Modred was seen by many as the good guy who slew the overmighty warlord?

Folklore connections

Whatever the historical legacy of the 'real' Arthur, his impact on the peoples of Britain has been immense. Hundreds of places have been named after him, and within the South-West alone there are numerous recorded folktales involving Arthur or his knights.

So numerous are these associations that I have selected from them according to the attractiveness and interest of the places rather than any supposed 'authenticity'.

In some cases it is very clear to us today that the connection with Arthur is fanciful, for example Trethevy Quoit north of Liskeard used to be called King Arthur's Quoit, but it is actually a very impressive Neolithic chambered tomb. Further north on Bodmin Moor lie 'King Arthur's Downs', and who can prove that Arthur never hunted there? On these Downs you can find King Arthur's Hall, a quite extraordinary structure, presumably prehistoric, so unusual that no archaeologist seems prepared to say what it might be – except that it certainly has no connection with Arthur. The name arose because a rectangular bank surrounds an enclosure the size of a large medieval hall, with stones placed vertically around the inner edge of the bank – and these stones can be fancifully interpreted as the chair-backs of Arthur's knights.

Natural as well as man-made features were named after Arthur: a flat outcrop of granite on Bodmin Moor is known as Arthur's Bed, for no reason at all that I can determine. Arthur's Oven and Arthur's Chair, possibly on Dartmoor, were shown to visitors as early as AD 1113.

The folklore stories may on the whole be later in origin than these namings of features. Quite a few involve ghostly visitations. For example Arthur and his knights are said to ride over 'King Arthur's Hunting Causeway', an ancient track (now unidentifiable, it seems) said to have run from South Cadbury to Glastonbury, and also to ride down a track to Sutton Montis, where their horses drink at a ford (see page 21).

The path at South Cadbury which once led to Sutton Montis – where you just might see the ghosts of King Arthur and his knights!

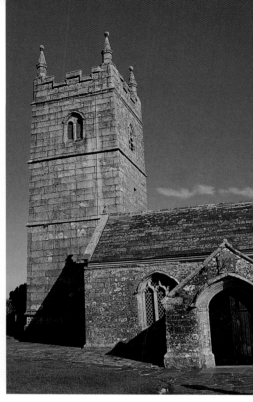

Left: Blackingstone Rock near Moretonhampstead, Devon

St Endellion church on the North Cornwall coast

There are numerous Arthur associations in both Somerset and Cornwall, but almost all trace of him seems to have disappeared from Devon, except for Blackingstone Rock near Moretonhampstead, an impressive tor rising out of luxuriant vegetation, on which Arthur apparently once met the devil.

In Cornwall near Tintagel lies the hamlet of Bossiney where there is a strange mound, probably the remains of a small castle motte though it may have started life as a burial mound. We are told that 'According to Cornish tradition King Arthur's Round Table lies deep in the earth under this earthen circular mound; only on Midsummer night does it rise, and then the flash of light from it for a moment illuminates the sky, after which the golden table sinks again…'

A very beautiful church at St Endellion, near Port Isaac on

Cornwall's north coast, has a legend concerning its patron, St Endelienta. Around 1600 Nicholas Roscarrock recorded the tale using the words '…as old people speaking by tradition do report'.

Endelienta was a food faddist who lived solely on cow's milk. One day her cow strayed onto a neighbour's land and the neighbour killed the cow. The saint's godfather was King Arthur, who promptly killed the neighbour. Endelienta thought this excessive, and restored her neighbour to life.

If godfather Arthur here sounds like a *mafioso*, perhaps that is true to life. Local chieftains and petty kings at that time were warriors who undertook the 'protection' of their people and in return claimed a substantial share of the local economy. That is how society worked from the Iron Age to late medieval times, with a brief respite during the Roman period.

St Endellion is within sight of Tintagel on a clear day, and it is perhaps appropriate that we return there at the end of this book, and take a look at Merlin's Cave, named after Arthur's mentor, the enigmatic wizard. This is a very atmospheric cavern which extends right through under the neck of land which divides the two parts of the castle. One day it will collapse, making the 'Island' truly an island. The cave has to be explored at low tide, as the sea fills it at other times.

Although Merlin's Rock at Mousehole was already so named by Tudor times, the name Merlin's Cave was probably created by Edwin Richards or his daughter Florence Nightingale Richards, who earned their living acting as guides to the castle in the nineteenth century. They were probably also responsible for other names on the Island, such as King Arthur's Footstep, King Arthur's Chair and even King Arthur's Cups and Saucers. Only the teaspoons are missing.

When the folklore collector Robert Hunt visited Tintagel in 1863, he 'sought with some anxiety for some stories of the British king, but not one could be obtained.' By the end of the century, the Richards family had rectified that.

The progressive embellishment of old stories, whether by medieval minstrels, Victorian guides or modern journalists, is now part of the process of folklore, which cannot be relied upon

'Merlin's Cave' at Tintagel. Geoffrey of Monmouth, who was so influential in spreading the Arthur story, also wrote about Merlin – who, like Arthur, may possibly have been a real person. If so, it seems he was from the North of Britain and became distraught when his people were cut down in a great battle

even for clues about historical fact. In the case of Arthur, alas, not a single one of the genuinely historical sources can be relied upon for historical fact either!

But this should not stop us from enjoying in their own right the many very beautiful and fascinating places with which Arthur's name has become connected.

Some other books

Arthurian Sites in the West C A Ralegh Radford and Michael J Swanton (University of Exeter Press)
Arthur's Britain, Leslie Alcock (Penguin)
Guinevere, the Grail, and all that, Paul White (Bossiney Books)
King Arthur, Man or Myth, Paul White (Bossiney Books)
The Life of Merlin, Geoffrey of Monmouth (Bossiney Books)
The Quest for Arthur's Britain, ed. Geoffrey Ashe (Paladin)

If King Arthur was a real historical figure, then he almost certainly lived much of his life in Dumnonia – the post-Roman kingdom which included Cornwall, Devon and part of Somerset and which was gradually whittled away until only Cornwall was left independent.

In this book Paul White explores places across the south-west traditionally associated with Arthur, some more plausibly than others, and recommends which are most likely to provide an enjoyable visit – for their intrinsic interest and beauty as well as for their Arthurian connections.

£2.99   Bossiney Books

ISBN 1-899383-52-2

9 781899 383528